The Holy Spirit

The Lutheran Difference Series

Korey Maas

CONCORDIA PUBLISHING HOUSE • SAINT LOUIS

3558 S. Jefferson Ave., St. Louis, MO 63118-3968
1-800-325-3040 • www.cph.org

Written by Korey Maas

Edited by Edward Engelbrecht

This publication may be available in braille, in large print, or on cassette tape for the visually impaired. Please allow 8 to 12 weeks for delivery. Write to the Library for the Blind, 1333 S. Kirkwood Road, St. Louis, MO 63122-7295; call 1-800-433-3954, ext. 1322; or e-mail to blind.library@lcms.org.

3 4 5 6 7 8 9 10 11 13 12 11 10 09 08

Contents

About This Series

"Are you filled with the Holy Spirit?"

"Sure . . . well, aren't all Christians filled with the Holy Spirit?"

As Lutherans interact with other Christians, they often find themselves struggling to explain their beliefs and practices. Although many Lutherans have learned the "what" of the doctrines of the church, they do not always have a full scriptural foundation to share the "why." When confronted with different doctrines, they cannot clearly state their faith, much less understand the differences.

Because of insecurities about explaining particular doctrines or practices, some Lutherans may avoid opportunities to share what they have learned from Christ and His Word. The Lutheran Difference Bible study series will identify how Lutherans differ from other Christians and show from the Bible why Lutherans differ. These studies will prepare Lutherans to share their faith and help non-Lutherans understand the Lutheran difference.

Student Introduction

Even in our increasingly irreligious society, people continue to talk about God, often in terms of His Fatherhood. The general public recognizes the name, person, and work of Jesus Christ. But what do those outside the church know of the third person of the Trinity? What do those *inside* the church know about the Holy Spirit?

The Lutheran church is perhaps especially open to the charge of "neglecting" the Holy Spirit. While one will not hear a Lutheran pastor preach even the shortest sermon without proclaiming Christ, Lutheran preaching often does not explicitly mention the Holy Spirit. Though this may be noted and criticized at times, Lutherans can say truthfully—if perhaps somewhat surprisingly—that it is neither an oversight nor an accident. Rather, it is entirely in keeping with Scripture's depiction of the office and work of the Spirit Himself.

As Jesus proclaimed to His disciples before His departure, the Spirit's task will be to "remind you of everything I have said to you" (John 14:26) and to "bring glory to Me" (John 16:14). The third person of the Trinity has no desire to draw attention to Himself; He has instead been sent for the purpose of directing our attention to God's saving work in Christ. In this regard Dr. Martin Luther explained: "That then is the Holy Spirit's office and work, that He through the gospel reveal what great and glorious thing God has done for us through Christ, namely, ransomed us from sin, death, and the power of the devil, received us into his grace and care, and given us himself wholly and sufficiently" (*Auslegungen über den Evangelisten Johannes*, Weimar edition, vol. 28, p. 82).

Where Christ is preached, Lutherans rejoice to believe, teach, and confess that the Spirit is always present and active. Far from neglecting the Spirit, Lutherans praise, honor, and glorify Him as God. This occurs not only when they speak *about* Him, but especially when in humble silence they allow Him to speak *to* them, to reveal the Savior and proclaim His salvation.

An Overview of Christian Denominations

The following outline of Christian history will help you understand where the different denominations come from and how they are related to one another. Use this outline in connection with the "Comparisons" sections found throughout the study. Statements of belief for the different churches are drawn from their official confessional writings.

The Great Schism

Eastern Orthodox: On July 16, 1054, Cardinal Humbert entered the Cathedral of the Holy Wisdom in Constantinople just before the worship service. He stepped to the altar and left a letter condemning Michael Cerularius, patriarch of Constantinople. Cerularius responded by condemning the letter and its authors. In that moment, Christian churches of the east and west were severed from each other. Their disagreements centered on what bread could be used in the Lord's Supper and the addition of the filioque statement to the Nicene Creed.

The Reformation

Lutheran: On June 15, 1520, Pope Leo X wrote a letter condemning Dr. Martin Luther for his Ninety-five Theses. Luther's theses had challenged the sale of indulgences, a fund-raising effort to pay for the building of St. Peter's Cathedral in Rome. The letter charged Luther with heresy and threatened to excommunicate him if he did not retract his writings within 60 days. Luther replied by publicly burning the letter. Leo excommunicated him on January 3, 1521, and condemned all who agreed with Luther or supported his cause.

Reformed: In 1522 the preaching of Ulrich Zwingli in Zurich, Switzerland, convinced people to break their traditional Lenten fast. Also, Zwingli preached that priests should be allowed to marry. When local friars challenged these departures from medieval church practice, the Zurich Council supported Zwingli and agreed that the Bible should guide Christian doctrine and practice. Churches of the Reformed tradition include Presbyterians and Episcopalians.

Anabaptist: In January 1525 Conrad Grebel, a follower of Ulrich Zwingli, rebaptized Georg Blaurock. Blaurock began rebaptizing others and founded the Swiss Brethren. Their insistence on adult believers' Baptism distinguished them from other churches of the Reformation. Anabaptists attracted social extremists who advocated violence in the cause of Christ, complete pacifism, or communal living. Mennonite, Brethren, and Amish churches descend from this movement.

The Counter Reformation

Roman Catholic: When people call the medieval church "Roman Catholic," they make a common historical mistake. Roman Catholicism as we know it emerged after the Reformation. As early as 1518 Luther and other reformers had appealed to the pope and requested a council to settle the issue of indulgences. Their requests were hindered or denied for a variety of theological and political reasons. Finally, on December 13, 1545, 34 leaders from the churches who opposed the Reformation gathered at the invitation of Pope Paul III. They began the Council of Trent (1545–63), which established the doctrine and practice of Roman Catholicism.

Post-Reformation Movements

Baptist: In 1608 or 1609 John Smyth, a former pastor of the Church of England, baptized himself by pouring water over his head. He formed a congregation of English Separatists in Holland, who opposed the rule of bishops and infant Baptism. This marked the start of the English Baptist churches, which remain divided doctrinally over the theology of John Calvin (Particular Baptists) and Jacob Arminius (General Baptists). In the 1800s the Restoration Movement of Alexander Campbell, a former Presbyterian minister, adopted many Baptist teachings. These churches include the Disciples of Christ (Christian Churches) and the Churches of Christ.

Wesleyan: In 1729 John and Charles Wesley gathered with three other men to study the Scripture, receive Communion, and discipline one another according to the "method" laid down in the Bible. Later, John Wesley's preaching caused religious revivals in England and America. Methodists, Wesleyans, Nazarenes, and Pentecostals form the Wesleyan family of churches.

Liberal: In 1799 Friedrich Schleiermacher published *Addresses on Religion* in an attempt to make Christianity appealing to people influenced by rationalism. He argued that religion is not a body of doctrines, provable truths, or a system of ethics, but belongs to the realm of feelings. His ideas did not lead to the formation of a new denomination, but deeply influenced Christian thinking. Denominations most thoroughly affected by liberalism are the United Church of Christ, Disciples of Christ, and Unitarianism.

Lutheran Facts

All who worship the holy Trinity and trust in Jesus Christ for the forgiveness of sins are regarded by Lutherans as fellow Christians, despite denominational differences.

Lutheran churches first described themselves as *evangelische* or evangelical churches. Opponents of these churches called them *Lutheran* after Dr. Martin Luther, the sixteenth-century German church reformer.

Lutherans are not disciples of Dr. Martin Luther but disciples of Jesus Christ. They proudly accept the name Lutheran because they agree with Dr. Luther's teaching from the Bible, as summarized in Luther's Small Catechism.

Lutherans focus most specifically on the work of the Holy Spirit on particular holidays: Baptism of Our Lord Sunday, Second Sunday of Easter (Quasimodogenti), and Pentecost.

During the service of confirmation, Lutherans publicly confirm the work of the Spirit in a person's life. The service commemorates the work of the Spirit through Baptism and the Word, leading a person to publicly confess faith in Jesus.

During the service of confirmation, the pastor lays his hand on the confirmand's head and prays for the sevenfold gift of the Spirit as described in Isaiah 11:2.

During the ordination and installation of pastors, Lutherans call especially on the work and guidance of the Holy Spirit, who appoints men to the pastoral office (John 20:21–23; Acts 20:28).

During the 1970s Lutheran churches, like most churches, were affected by the charismatic movement. A small percentage of Lutherans claim special gifts of the Spirit. Most Lutherans emphasize the work of the Holy Spirit through the Word of God rather than through specially anointed individuals.

Lutherans worship and pray to the Holy Spirit as the third person of the Holy Trinity.

To prepare for "The Spirit Speaks," read 1 Corinthians 2:6–16.

The Spirit Speaks

Sticks and stones may break my bones,
but words can never hurt me.

—A nursery rhyme

Words. Are they really so powerless? Mere scribbles and sound bites can stop a dispute or end a friendship. Words can begin a marriage or begin a war. Stronger even than human speech are the words that proceed from the mouth of God. Thankfully, unlike so many of our words, God's strong Word was written—and is still preached—for our benefit.

1. What are some of the various reasons, both positive and negative, that people have for speaking with one another? For what reason might God feel it necessary or desirable to verbally speak with those He has created?

Discerning Spirit

2. Read Psalm 33:6 and 2 Peter 3:5. Compare Hebrews 4:12 and Ephesians 6:17. What do these passages say about words that come from God's mouth? What makes these words do what they do?

God's Word moves more than molecules of air and stirs more than breath. His Word can move and stir the heart.

The Spirit continued to speak through the words of the New Testament apostles. (See, for example, Acts 1:2 and 1 Corinthians 2:12–13. See especially 2 Peter 3:15–16, which ascribes to the words of the apostle Paul authority equal to that of the prophets.) As will be discussed below, the Spirit inspired the authors of both the Old and New Testaments to reveal Him who stands at the center of all Scripture—Christ, whose life and death won our salvation.

3. God spoke His creation into being, but divine speech did not end there. Read 2 Peter 1:21 and 2 Timothy 3:16. Who is described as speaking in these passages? To whom does God speak? For what purpose?

4. While rejoicing that God would speak to His creation in human language, Christians also realize that some readers have difficulty understanding the Bible. Read 1 Corinthians 2:14 and 2 Corinthians 3:15–16. What do these passages say about the role of the Spirit in understanding God's Word?

The Spirit proclaims both Law and Gospel. Though He must convict and condemn, the Spirit's "proper" work is to proclaim Christ.

5. To understand Scripture—or any literature—requires an awareness of its major themes. Read Nehemiah 9:30 and John 16:7–8. Compare these with Titus 3:5 and John 20:22–23. According to these passages, how is the work of the Holy Spirit related to the biblical themes of Law and Gospel?

So intimately and essentially related are the Spirit and the preaching of Christ, Luther was led to declare in the Large Catechism that "where Christ is not preached, there is no Holy Ghost" ("The Creed," Art. III.45).

6. Jesus declared that the Scriptures testify about Him (John 5:39). Compare John 14:26 and 16:13–14. According to Jesus, what do

the testimony of Scripture and the testimony of the Holy Spirit have in common?

7. Though the Holy Spirit speaks and acts through God's external Word, there are spirits who do not do so. Read 1 John 4:1. What warning and exhortation does the author give? How might this exhortation be observed?

Word and Spirit

The Holy Spirit not only inspired the ancient and original authors of the Bible; He works even today through the external Word, continuing to fulfill God's holy will.

8. How might understanding the emphases and intent of the Holy Spirit's inspiration of Scripture affect your attitude toward and approach to the study of the Bible?

9. What comfort can you take in knowing that where God's Word is, there also is the Holy Spirit?

Sure Word

Where God's Word is, there also is His Spirit. Not only is He present; He is active, and powerfully too. Acting through the Word of Scripture, He continually—and convincingly—convicts us of sin. But thanks be to God, He also pardons us for the sake of Christ.

10. How might the way God has spoken to you through His Word affect the manner in which you speak to Him in prayer?

11. How might you respond to a friend who believes that God has spoken—or wonders if God has spoken—to him or her through means other than the revealed Word of Scripture?

Comparisons

Verbal Inspiration: The Holy Spirit led the prophets, evangelists, and apostles to write the books of the Bible. He guided their writing, inspiring their very words while working through their particular styles of expression. Therefore, the Bible's words are God's Word. Conservative Christian churches hold this view. Many also maintain that the original writings of the Bible were without error (inerrancy) but some mistakes entered the text as the scribes copied, edited, or translated the Scripture over the centuries.

Partial Inspiration: Christians affected by theological liberalism hold different views of the inspiration of the Bible. For example, some would assert that the Bible is God's Word but the authors erred in some factual details. Others would say that the Bible contains God's Word and the Spirit leads people today to determine which parts of the Bible God wants them to follow. Still others would say that the Bible is one testimony to God's Word along with writings used in other religions.

Inspired Translations: Some churches hold that God inspired certain translations of the Bible. For example, the Eastern Orthodox church holds that the Greek Septuagint translation of the Old Testament was inspired by God. Some English-speaking Protestants hold that God inspired the King James translation of the Bible.

To prepare for "The Spirit of God," read John 15:26–16:16.

The Spirit of God

Your life and the world you live in will never be the same.

—the character "Trinity," from the film *The Matrix*

Trinity. Christians hear this word so often they may sometimes fail to appreciate its true meaning. *Coequal, coeternal*: Christians use these words so little that they may not even know what they mean! The Holy Trinity is, to be sure, a great mystery. What's more, the third person of the Trinity, the Holy Spirit, may be the most mysterious.

12. In your own words, describe the person and work of the Holy Spirit. What is His relation to the Father and Son? To the Christian? To the Christian church?

A Personal Being

13. Read Psalm 139:7–10 and 1 Corinthians 2:10–11. What attributes do these passages ascribe to the Holy Spirit? What does this tell you about the nature of the Spirit?

Jesus professes in John 4:24 that "God is Spirit," while Paul declares even more clearly in 2 Corinthians 3:17 that "the Lord is the Spirit." Based on such evidence, the church confesses in the Athanasian Creed her belief that "the Father is God, the Son is God, and the Holy Spirit is God."

14. Many people, when hearing the word *spirit*, think of an impersonal energy or "life force." Read Isaiah 63:10 and Romans

15:30. Compare Acts 13:2 and 1 Corinthians 2:13; 12:11. Rather than an impersonal energy, how do the biblical authors describe the Spirit?

But what exactly does it mean to use the term *person* in reference to the Holy Spirit? The authors of the Athanasian Creed confessed that "there is one Person of the Father, another of the Son, and another of the Holy Ghost." Commenting on this and other testimonies of the early Christian church, the Lutheran Reformers insisted that "the term 'person' [should be used] as the Fathers have used it, to signify, not a part or quality in another, but that which subsists of itself" (AC I). That is, the Spirit is not merely a part of God or God's energy; He is God Himself.

15. Read Acts 5:3–4; 2 Corinthians 13:14; and Matthew 28:19. How do Peter, Paul, and even Jesus Himself confess the Christian belief that the Holy Spirit is truly God, yet a person distinct from both the Father and the Son?

Given the mystery of the Trinity, it is not surprising that there was much argument in the early church about the exact nature of the relationship between Father, Son, and Holy Spirit. Much of the debate focused on terms such as *begotten* and *proceeds,* words we know today from the creeds formulated during those early controversies.

16. Though it is impossible for human reason to understand how three persons are one God and one God is three persons, Scripture is not silent about this mystery. Read John 15:26. Compare Matthew 10:20 with Galatians 4:6. What do such passages say about the relationship of the Holy Spirit to the Father and Son from eternity and within the Trinity itself?

The Bible not only describes the relationship of the Spirit to the Father and Son with regard to their essence and being; it also describes this relationship as it applies to their work in the world and for the world. It is common, and certainly not incorrect, to classify the work of the Father as creation, that of the Son as redemption, and that of the Holy Spirit as sanctification (see, for example, Luther's introduction to the Apostles' Creed in his Large Catechism). It would be an error, however, to *limit* the work of the three persons of the Trinity to these works, possibly giving the impression that the work of each is unrelated to the work of the others.

17. Read and compare John 1:18 and John 16:14. How is the work of the Spirit related to that of the Father and the Son?

Jesus explains to the Samaritan woman that God must be worshiped according to His nature. Because "God is spirit," Jesus explains, He must be worshiped "in spirit." Likewise, because God and His Word—both the written and incarnate Word (cf. John 14:6 and 17:17)—are truth, God is to be worshiped "in truth."

18. Read John 4:23–24. On the basis of the above passages, how would you describe worship that takes place "in spirit and truth"?

A Personal Faith

Christians do not merely believe in "spirit," but in *the* Spirit, the Holy Spirit, the third person of the Trinity, God Himself. This biblical faith offers the believer great comfort.

19. What comfort can be found in knowing that the Holy Spirit is not merely a spiritual substance or energy, but a divine person?

When tempted by the spirits of the world, we are reassured to know that the Spirit of God never ceases His work of creating and strengthening faith, bringing forgiveness in Word and Sacraments, and directing our lives in accordance with the will of God.

20. As you reflect on your personal faith, worship, and life, what consolation and encouragement does the adjective *holy*, as applied to God's Spirit, provide?

Mystery and Revelation

The mystery of the holy Trinity is incomprehensible to human reason. Nevertheless, it is true, as God's true Word declares. Though we are unable to comprehend the "how," we joyfully confess the "who" of the Trinity: Father, Son, and Holy Spirit.

21. Think of ways in which you might answer a friend who questions the nature of the Holy Spirit and His relation to God the Father and God the Son.

22. In what ways can you, in your personal devotional life, more frequently and consciously confess the divinity of the Holy Spirit?

Comparisons

Proceeds from the Father and the Son: Christians of the western tradition teach that the Holy Spirit proceeds from the Father *and the Son* (*filioque* in Latin). They tend to emphasize the coequal divinity of the Father, Son, and Holy Spirit.

Proceeds from the Father: Eastern Orthodox churches have never accepted the *filioque* statement added by western churches to the Nicene Creed. They contend that the Spirit proceeds from the Father *through* the Son, emphasizing more of a hierarchy among the persons of the Trinity.

Pseudo-Christian Beliefs: A variety of groups reject the divinity of the Holy Spirit and the doctrine of the Trinity. For example, the Jehovah's Witnesses regard the Holy Spirit as an impersonal force. The United Pentecostal church teaches that the Father, Son, and Holy Spirit are all manifestations of the same person ("Jesus only"). Mormons hold that the Holy Spirit is a spiritual god alongside the Father and the Son, who are gods with physical bodies.

To prepare for "Life-giving Spirit," read Romans 8:1–17.

Life-giving Spirit

In Your radiance
Life from heaven now is given overflowing,
Gift of gifts beyond all knowing.

—Michael Schirmer, *LW* 160

Every day we make choices. Sometimes we clamor for more options from which to choose; sometimes we wish there were not so many options. Whether or not we enjoy them—or even notice them—each and every day our lives are filled with countless choices. How strange, then, that none of us made the first and most important decision: to begin our own life.

23. In what matters or on what occasions do you sometimes wish you had more choices? Are there times you wish you had to make fewer choices? Why?

Breath of God

24. Read Genesis 1:2; 2:7; and Job 33:4. To what do these passages refer? Who is involved?

25. Read Ephesians 2:1 and Acts 7:51. What do these passages say about the once-holy creation into which God breathed life?

26. Being dead in trespasses, the sinner must be reborn or re-created if he or she is to have life. Read Psalm 51:10 and Psalm 104:29–30. Compare John 3:3–5 and Romans 8:11. What do these passages say about rebirth and re-creation? What is the source of new life?

New life is given only on account of the life sacrificed by Christ. In this life given for us, the Holy Spirit played a prominent role.

27. Read Luke 1:35 and 3:21–22. Compare John 15:26 and 16:13–14. How does the Spirit's activity at the beginning of Jesus' earthly life relate to that mentioned near the end of Jesus' ministry?

The life of Jesus, the life given into death for our sins, is the one and only basis for our salvation. That we might know of His glorious work on our behalf, the Spirit has been given as His witness. For this we must truly give thanks.

28. Not only does the Spirit play a role in the life of Jesus; He is also involved in our own lives. Read 1 Corinthians 6:11. What activities are here attributed to the Holy Spirit?

29. "Justification by faith" is a phrase familiar to Lutherans. Read 1 Corinthians 12:3. What is the relationship described here between faith and the Holy Spirit? (See also pages 61–62.)

Lively Spirit

The Holy Spirit acts without our asking, without our effort, and at times without our knowledge. But knowing how and for what purpose the Spirit is active can be a source of great comfort and encouragement for the Christian.

Christians are not immune to feelings of insignificance, meaninglessness, or loneliness. The modern world teaches a "closed universe." God—if He exists at all—does not intervene in our lives. This teaching leaves people alone to question their life's meaning and purpose. It certainly does nothing to alleviate such negative thoughts.

30. What comfort do you take knowing that God's Spirit has been active in the world from the time of creation and continues to act on your behalf even today?

31. Knowing that the Holy Spirit's work is to testify to Christ, how might you be encouraged in your own evangelism efforts?

Live in the Spirit

Acting through Word and Sacraments, the Spirit testifies to the person and work of Jesus Christ. What is more, through these means the Holy Spirit not only points to our salvation in Christ, but He effects our salvation! Without our cooperation, He raises us from death in sin to new life in Christ.

32. Knowing that life—and new life—are free gifts of the Spirit, how might you show your thanks in your worship and devotional life?

The biblical parallels between creation and re-creation, birth and rebirth, speak against the notion that we must in some way cooperate with the Holy Spirit's work of justification.

33. In light of your study, how might you respond to a friend who believes that one must "make a decision" or otherwise work with the Spirit in salvation?

Comparisons

As you read the following comparison quotes or summaries, look for how the different churches talk about the work of the Holy Spirit, whether through the means of grace or within a person.

Eastern Orthodox: "Is the Holy Ghost communicated to men even now likewise? He is communicated to all true Christians. . . . How may we be made partakers of the Holy Ghost? Through fervent prayer, and through the Sacraments" (*Longer Catechism of the Eastern Church*, questions 249–250).

Lutheran: "I believe that I cannot by my own reason or strength believe in Jesus Christ, my Lord, or come to Him; but the Holy Spirit has called me by the Gospel, enlightened me with His gifts, sanctified and kept me in the true faith" (Luther's Small Catechism, "The Creed," art. III). Lutherans emphasize that the Holy Spirit works through the means of grace: the Word and Sacraments.

Reformed: "But when God accomplishes His good pleasure in the elect, or works in them true conversion, He not only causes the gospel to be externally preached to them, and powerfully illuminates their minds by His Holy Spirit . . . but by the efficacy of the same regenerating Spirit He pervades the inmost recesses of the man" (*Canons of the Synod of Dort*, Art. XI).

Roman Catholic: The Holy Spirit awakens faith in unbelievers and communicates new life to them through the ministry of the church.

Anabaptist: This movement emphasizes the mystical work of the Spirit in the heart rather than through Word and Sacraments. Only holy people have received the Holy Spirit and are members of the church.

Baptist: "We believe that Repentance and Faith are sacred duties, and also inseparable graces, wrought in our souls by the regenerating Spirit of God" (*New Hampshire Baptist Confession*).

Wesleyan: "But as soon as he is born of God . . . he is now capable of hearing the inward voice of God, saying, 'Be of good cheer; thy sins are forgiven thee'; 'Go and sin no more.' . . . He 'feels in his heart,' to use the language of our Church, 'the mighty working of the Spirit of God'" (*Standard Sermons of John Wesley*, XXXIX.4).

To prepare for "The Spirit of Holiness," read John 16:12–15; 17:13–19.

The Spirit of Holiness

The gods help those who help themselves.

—Aesop's Fables

Whether it be through "twelve steps" or "seven habits," it seems that everyone—both in and out of the church—is engaging in some sort of self-help or self-improvement. We want to look better, feel better, and act better. But even our so-called self-help is rarely done by ourselves. We enlist the aid of books, support groups, and personal trainers.

34. What drives our constant desire to better ourselves? Why do you think the market for self-help books and programs is so large?

The Helpless Self

35. Working through the Scripture, the Holy Spirit fulfills the purpose of Scripture: bringing sinners to salvation. Read and compare Romans 15:4 and 2 Timothy 3:16–17. For what other purpose does the Spirit work through the Word of God?

Since even those forgiven by Christ continue to struggle with the effects of original sin, we are not yet the perfectly pure and holy people our gracious God first created us to be. Thus, Martin Luther wrote in his Large Catechism that "For now we are only half pure and holy, so that the Holy Ghost has ever [some reason why] to continue His work in us through the Word, and daily to dispense forgiveness, until we attain to that life where there will be no more forgiveness, but only perfectly pure and holy people, full of godliness and righteousness, removed and free from sin, death, and all evil, in a new, immortal, and glorified body."

36. Read Romans 8:12–13 and 2 Corinthians 3:18. In what terms does Paul describe the Spirit's work of sanctification?

Sanctification is daily putting to death sin and being transformed into the likeness of our holy God.

37. Read John 17:17; 1 Corinthians 6:11; and 1 Thessalonians 5:23–24. In these passages, who brings about sanctification? How does this happen?

We are sanctified by the truth, which is God's own Word, the means through which the Spirit is always at work. It is by the power of God's Word that the church is called into existence, sins are forgiven, and eternal life is granted. Hence the words of the Large Catechism: "I believe that the Holy Ghost makes me holy, as His name implies. But whereby does He accomplish this, or what are His method and means to this end? Answer: By the Christian Church, the forgiveness of sins, the resurrection of the body, and the life everlasting."

38. Read 1 Corinthians 12:13 and Ephesians 2:19–22. What does each passage describe, and how does it relate to the work of the Holy Spirit?

The Spirit's presence and activity are in fact the only basis on which the church can rightly be called holy. The church is not always in its outward and visible life more holy than other organizations. Without the Holy Spirit, there is no holy Christian church. (See pages 58–59.)

39. Prayer is associated with the sanctified Christian life. Read Ephesians 6:18 and Jude 20. What does each say about prayer? Compare to Romans 8:26–27.

40. The Christian's sanctification is not limited to deeds that seem outwardly holy. Read Exodus 31:1–5 and 35:30–33. Why was the Spirit given? In what sense can this be said to effect sanctification?

The examples from Exodus may seem strange until we realize that "good works" are merely works done by "good people," that is, those having been declared holy and good by God Himself. The Christian is doing the will of God, living out the life of sanctification, when he or she faithfully carries out the tasks of his or her vocations. The many callings we have received—pastor or parishioner, parent or child, employer or employee—are, when carried out faithfully, means by which our neighbor is loved and served. For this reason, Martin Luther appended to his Small Catechism a Table of Duties, concluding them with reference to Romans 13:8, "he who loves his fellowman has fulfilled the law."

Ever-present Help

41. In Leviticus 19:2 the Lord's people are told: "Be holy because I, the LORD your God, am holy." That's a tall order! What consolation do you receive from being assured that the Spirit Himself is continuously at work, making the people of God a holy people?

42. What comfort do you take in knowing that the Spirit constantly prays for you?

43. Aside from participating in worship, many Christians do not find time to be actively involved in the affairs of the church. What encouragement may you receive knowing that your sanctification is being worked out even in your profession, your family, and other areas of life?

Beyond Self-Help

The Christian's sanctification, we can joyously confess, is no mere matter of self-help. God assures us that He has not only declared us holy, but that His Holy Spirit is constantly at work in us, with us, and through us to make us holy.

44. How might you respond to a friend who attempts to simplify the Christian experience by claiming that God works our justification, but we must work our own sanctification?

45. Set aside some time in your daily devotions to read the Table of Duties in Luther's Small Catechism. Ask yourself how your sanctification is being worked out in each of your various vocations. In your prayers, include petitions asking that you might be strengthened to faithfully carry out these vocations.

Comparisons

Since the Reformation, the confessional writings of Christians have generally agreed that sanctification or holiness is a result of God's justifying grace in Christ. However, different traditions emphasize different teachings about holiness based on their views of sin and the abilities of the human will.

Perfect Holiness Only in Heaven: Lutherans, the Reformed, and many Baptists teach that Christians do not attain perfection in this life because of the taint of original sin. The Holy Spirit sanctifies believers in lives of greater service to God and others.

Degrees of Holiness: Roman Catholics and the Eastern Orthodox church teach that the saints attain a greater degree of holiness than most Christians. They attain this through fervent prayer, good works, and self-deprivation. Roman Catholics also teach that Mary was born without the taint of original sin.

Perfectionism: Churches of the Wesleyan and Anabaptist traditions teach that it is possible to reach a state of perfection. Perfection is a second work of grace following justification and is usually accompanied by a mystical, personal experience.

Ethics: Liberalism emphasizes personal or corporate standards of conduct, which the human will can attain through love and discipline.

To prepare for "Baptized with the Spirit," read Acts 1:1–9.

Baptized with the Spirit

The Word by seers or sibyls told,
In groves of oak, or fares of gold,
Still floats upon the morning wind,
Still whispers to the willing mind.
One accent of the Holy Ghost
The heedless world hath never lost.

—Ralph Waldo Emerson, *The Problem*

Emerson's poetry signaled an important shift in American religious thought, away from the words of Scripture toward "natural" spirituality.

Human beings reveal strange inner contrasts. We waver between the emotional and the empirical. At times we just want to feel things, and at times we want definitely to know things. Sometimes we want an internal experience, and sometimes we want external proof. Unfortunately, these otherwise wonderful impulses—as with all human inclinations—can confuse or mislead.

46. Can you think of times when you may have ignored what seemed obviously to be true just because it didn't "feel right"? Are there some instances when it may be inappropriate to demand hard evidence for something?

The Promised Spirit

47. Read Joel 2:28–29 and John 7:39. What promise does the Lord give in Joel? For whom is this promise made? When was God's promise fulfilled?

48. Read and compare Mark 1:8 and 1 Corinthians 12:13. What activity or event is mentioned in each passage? Who is involved in each?

While some may not even realize they have been baptized with the Spirit (see 1 Corinthians 3:16), and while some may show little evidence of the Spirit—as was the case in the carnal Corinthian church—Paul writes quite emphatically that "if anyone does not have the Spirit of Christ, he does not belong to Christ" (Romans 8:9). That is, if one has not received the Spirit, one is not a Christian.

49. Read Acts 10:43–44 and Galatians 3:2. By what means is the Holy Spirit received?

50. Compare Romans 8:9–11 with 1 Corinthians 12:3. How do these passages describe the relationship between Christ and the Holy Spirit? Are the two separable?

51. Read Romans 6:3–4 and 1 Peter 3:21. How do these passages describe the relationship between Christ and Baptism? Are the two separable?

52. Read Ephesians 4:3–6. Compare Matthew 16:4 with 1 Corinthians 1:22–23. How might such passages serve to warn the church against placing an undue emphasis on a second "baptism in the Spirit"?

While Paul makes clear that the church recognizes only one Baptism, the value of this Baptism sometimes comes into question if the Spirit's presence and activity are not always or explicitly felt and seen. What is often sought is an obvious manifestation of the Spirit, such as prophesying, speaking in tongues, or healing. Against placing too much confidence in one's senses, however, both Jesus and Paul warn that signs are not to be demanded.

Comforting Spirit

Even before the birth of His Son, God promised that His Spirit would be poured out on all people. The promise of Joel, as with all Old Testament prophecies, has been fulfilled in Christ. It was He who sent the Spirit from His Father on Pentecost, and it is He whose name we are baptized into even today.

53. What encouragement is found in knowing that God's Old Testament promise has been fulfilled?

54. What consolation do you take in knowing that all Christians—even those as sin-steeped as the Corinthians—have been baptized in the Spirit?

55. Read Matthew 28:19. What comfort may it provide to know you have not been baptized in the Spirit alone, but into the name of the Trinity itself: Father, Son, *and* Holy Spirit?

Life in the Spirit

Quite frequently Christians do not feel holy inwardly. Just as often we appear outwardly unholy. We rejoice, therefore, to be assured that our holiness is not a matter of internal feelings or external evidence. Personal holiness rests upon God's Word and Spirit having, in our Baptism, declared and made it true.

56. What loving response could you give to those who might downplay your Baptism with water and the Word by asking, "Yes, but have you been baptized *with the Holy Spirit*?"

57. In your daily devotional life, what can you do to acknowledge and give thanks for the great blessings the Spirit has bestowed on you in your Baptism?

Comparisons

Eastern Orthodox: "Baptism is a Sacrament, in which a man who believes . . . dies to the carnal life of sin, and is born again of the Holy Ghost to a life spiritual and holy" (*Longer Catechism of the Eastern Church*, question 288).

Lutheran: "For without God's word the water is plain water and no Baptism. But with the word of God it is a Baptism, that is, a life-giving water, rich in grace, and a washing of new birth in the Holy Spirit" (Luther's Small Catechism, "Baptism," part III).

Reformed: "By the right use of this ordinance [Baptism] the grace promised is not only offered, but really exhibited and conferred by the Holy Ghost, to such (whether of age or infants) as that grace belongeth unto, according to the counsel of God's own will, in his appointed time" (*Westminster Confession of Faith*, chapter XXVIII.VI).

Anabaptist: "Concerning baptism we confess that penitent believers, who, through faith, regeneration, and the renewing of the Holy

Ghost, are made one with God, and are written in heaven, must, upon such Scriptural confession of faith, and renewing of life, be baptized with water" (*Dordrecht Confession* VII).

Roman Catholics: Baptism both signifies and causes the new birth of water and the Spirit.

Baptist: "Sinners must be regenerated or born again; that regeneration consists in giving a holy disposition to the mind; that it is effected in a manner above our comprehension by the power of the Holy Spirit, in connection with divine truth, so as to secure our voluntary obedience to the gospel" (*New Hampshire Baptist Confession*, Art. 7).

Wesleyan: "Baptism is not only a sign of profession and mark of difference whereby Christians are distinguished from others that are not baptized; but it is also a sign of regeneration, or the new birth" (*Methodist Articles of Religion*, XVII). Holiness churches and Pentecostals teach a second work of grace, after regeneration, by which God "perfects" a person or baptizes them in the Holy Spirit.

To prepare for "The Fruit and Gifts of the Spirit," read Isaiah 11:1–3a and Galatians 5:16–26.

The Fruit and Gifts of the Spirit

LORD, shall we not bring these gifts to Your service?
Shall we not bring to Your service all our powers?
For life, for dignity, grace and order,
And intellectual pleasures of the senses?

—T. S. Eliot, choruses from "The Rock"

Have you ever heard someone say, "She's at the top of her class, she sings in the choir, and she's captain of the swim team. She's really quite gifted."

We often hear teachers, counselors, and researchers speak of gifted children. And we certainly rejoice if they're talking about our children! But what about children who are not given the "gifted" label? Do they lack gifts?

58. As it is frequently used today, what does the term *gifted* mean? Is it a helpful or useful term? Why or why not?

God's Gifts

59. Read Galatians 5:22–24 and compare to Romans 8:22–23. What does Paul describe in these passages? How do such things relate to the Holy Spirit's work of sanctification?

On several occasions Paul discusses what are called "spiritual gifts." He lists these gifts as follows:

Romans 12:6–8	1 Corinthians 12:4–10	1 Corinthians 12:28
Serving	The message of wisdom	Apostleship
Teaching	The message of knowledge	Prophecy
Encouraging	Faith	Teaching
Contributing	Gifts of healing	Healing
Leading	Miraculous powers	Helping others
Showing mercy	Prophecy	Administration
Distinguishing spirits	Tongues	Interpreting tongues

In our own day there is frequent and often confusing discussion of spiritual gifts. The same was true even in the days of the apostles. Paul therefore begins his discussion in 1 Corinthians 12 by saying, "About spiritual gifts, brethren, I do not want you to be ignorant."

60. Of what, then, does Paul inform us? How do the lists of gifts compare with one another? Are the same things described in each passage?

It seems that Paul's purpose is *not* to give a definitive or exhaustive list of spiritual gifts. Instead, his purpose is to confirm that Christians do indeed have gifts given by God Himself and that the use of these gifts should not cause division in the church.

61. Read 1 Corinthians 12:7 and 1 Peter 4:10. For what purpose do Peter and Paul say spiritual gifts are given?

62. Read 1 Corinthians 1:7 and 1 Corinthians 12:7, 11. To whom are spiritual gifts given?

To be sure, we can use God's gifts selfishly or unwisely, as was the case in Corinth. We may also at times be unaware of the Holy Spirit's gifts—in ourselves and in others. This is because these manifestations are given by the Spirit "as He determines" and as He wills (1 Corinthians 12:7; cf. John 3:8). They may not always be obvious, especially when our sinfulness is! (See page 61.)

63. Reread the passages from the table on page 36. Are spiritual gifts necessarily supernatural endowments? Might they also be considered natural talents, though certainly God-given?

64. Read and compare John 3:8 and 1 Corinthians 12:11. What do these passages say about the manner in which the Holy Spirit works? Do these passages suggest that the same spiritual gifts will be given in all places at all times?

Christ instituted the means of grace as the unchanging instruments by which He provides for our *spiritual* needs, working both our justification and our sanctification. As means by which to serve the *material* needs of the church and her members, however, different gifts of the Spirit may be given as different circumstances require.

Gifts of Service

The Holy Spirit in whom Christians have been baptized has not only provided us with the free gift of salvation and eternal life in heaven; He also bestows on us many and various gifts to be used in service to the church on earth.

65. What encouragement is there in knowing that all those who have received the Holy Spirit in Baptism have also received His gifts?

66. In what ways is it comforting to know that the Spirit gives different gifts to different members of the Christian church?

Gifted Children

As God's sure Word declares, *all* of His children are gifted. Having received, we then also give. We give of our time and talent to serve others.

67. How might you respond to someone who questions those who do not exhibit some of the more spectacular gifts of the Spirit, such as speaking in tongues or miraculous healing?

68. Spiritual gifts are given to use in service to others. In your daily devotions, take time to thank God for the talents and abilities He has given you and other members in the church. How might your talents best be put into service in your own congregation?

Comparisons

Natural Gifts: God gives talents to all people (whether Christian or not) as part of the created order. Christians should use these gifts in service to the Creator and the church.

Spiritual Gifts: Pentecostals and Charismatics teach that special, miraculous gifts are normally part of every believer's life. They place special emphasis on "speaking in tongues" as a sign of receiving a "baptism with the Holy Spirit." Lutherans and other Christians have taught that the Holy Spirit bestows spiritual gifts through Baptism. The Eastern Orthodox church and Roman Catholics teach that the Holy Spirit bestows or strengthens spiritual gifts through confirmation.

Leader Guide

Leaders, please note the different abilities of your class members. Some will easily find the Bible passages listed in this study. Others will struggle. To make participation easier, team up members of the class. For example, if a question asks you to look up several passages, assign one passage to one group, the second to another, and so on. Divide up the work! Let participants present the different answers that they discover.

Each topic is divided into four easy-to-use sections.

Focus introduces key concepts that will be discovered.

Inform guides the participants into Scripture to uncover truths concerning a doctrine.

Connect enables participants to apply what is learned in Scripture to their lives and provides them an opportunity to formulate and articulate a defense of a key doctrine.

Vision provides participants with practical suggestions for extending the theme of the lesson out of the classroom and into the world.

Also take note of the Comparisons section at the end of each lesson. The editor has drawn this material from the official confessional documents and historical works of the various denominations. The passages describe and compare the denominations so that students can see how Lutherans differ from other Christians and also see how all Christians share many of the same beliefs and practices. The passages are not polemical.

The Spirit Speaks

Objectives

By the power of the Holy Spirit working through God's Word, participants will (1) describe the relationship between God's Word and its divine Author, (2) recognize the common testimony of both Spirit and Word—our salvation in Christ Jesus, and (3) know that where God's Word is, there also His Spirit is active.

Opening Worship

Sing "God Has Spoken by His Prophets" (*LW* 343).

Focus

1. Read, or ask a participant to read aloud, the opening paragraph. Discuss the nature and purpose of communication. Why do we communicate? Are some forms of communication better suited than others for certain purposes? Allow participants to offer suggestions regarding the question of why God may have felt it necessary or desirable to communicate with humans and why He may have chosen to communicate by the particular means He has chosen, the external, written Word of Scripture.

Discerning Spirit (Inform)

2. The authors of the Old and New Testaments are in complete agreement: the heavens and the earth were created by God. They are also in agreement regarding the manner in which He created. Out of nothing, God *spoke* the universe into being. The spoken word of God is a tremendously powerful thing; it is, as the author of Hebrews calls it, "living and active." How can mere words do such things? Of course, they are not "mere" words; they are God's own words. They are living and active because the Spirit lives in them and acts through them. They are, in the language of St. Paul, the Spirit's "sword"—the powerful tool or instrument by which the Spirit carries out His divine work.

3. St. Peter declares that although the prophets spoke and wrote to God's people, they did not do so of their own accord. They spoke "from God," being "carried along by the Holy Spirit." Paul echoes this thought as he writes to the young pastor Timothy, saying, "all Scripture is God-breathed." Such passages proclaim the doctrine of Scripture's inspiration. Though Scripture does not explain the precise manner in which it was inspired, it teaches that its words come from God Himself through the Spirit.

4. Our understanding of the written Word of Scripture could not take place without the Spirit's activity. This is St. Paul's point when he writes: "The man without the Spirit does not accept the things that come from the Spirit . . . and he cannot understand them." Writing again to the Corinthians, he further explains by way of illustration. There are some, he says, who read Scripture as though a veil were draped between them and its true meaning. But with the Spirit "the veil is taken away."

5. Believing that the Holy Spirit inspired Scripture and works through it, the Old and New Testament authors speak also of the Spirit's work in terms of Law and Gospel. Nehemiah, for example, records a prayer of the Levites in which the Spirit is said to have admonished Israel. Likewise, Jesus announces in John 16 that the Spirit will "convict the world of guilt."

The work of the Spirit has not only to do with the Law, however. St. Paul assures us that the Gospel is very much the concern of the Spirit. "He saved us," Paul writes to Titus, "through the washing of rebirth and renewal by the Holy Spirit." This rebirth and renewal through the forgiveness of sins is, as seen in John 20, the specific purpose for which the Holy Spirit was bestowed upon the apostles.

6. Jesus declared that the Scriptures testify about Him (John 5:39). Likewise, Jesus ascribes this work to the Holy Spirit. The Spirit will remind the disciples of all that Jesus has said (John 14:26) and will bring glory to Him (John 16:14).

7. The knowledge that God's Spirit is constantly working through God's Word offers great assurance to the Christian. But, as John notes in his first letter, there also exist false spirits, those who are not God's. Therefore, be on guard, always testing the spirits and those who speak by them. But how? The intimate relationship between the Holy Spirit and Holy Scripture provides the basis on which to test the spirits. That is, if a spirit seems to call, gather, or enlighten and yet does so without the Word of God, it is not the Spirit of God. (See page 62.)

Word and Spirit (Connect)

8. Knowing the Holy Spirit's purpose in revealing God's Word helps us to properly read and understand it. As Jesus declared, the Scriptures testify to Him (John 5:39; see also John 20:31). Understanding this, we read Scripture knowing that in all its parts it speaks of our salvation in Christ—and our need for salvation.

9. The Scriptures have been written for your salvation. However, this is far from all that Scripture has to offer. It not only speaks about your salvation; it *affects* your personal salvation. The external Word of Scripture, in which the Holy Spirit is living and active, is the means by which God forgives your sin and declares you to be His child. God promises that His Word "will accomplish what I desire and achieve the purpose for which I sent it" (Isaiah 55:11).

Sure Word (Vision)

10. That God's Spirit has called, gathered, enlightened, and sanctified us by means of His Word prompts us, when speaking to Him in worship and prayer, to offer heartfelt praise and thanksgiving. Also, knowing that His Word offers a clear and truthful expression of His holy will, we are often stimulated to worship and pray using His own words, saying back to Him what He has already said to us.

11. Statements such as "I really think God is telling me to . . ." or "I feel that the Holy Spirit has laid it on my heart to . . ." are common expressions in some Christian churches. The problem, of course, is that if one only "thinks" or "feels," then there can be no certainty that it is God Himself who is speaking. Such certainty only comes when we look for God to speak where He has promised to do so—in His revealed, written Word. One manner in which we might respond to these statements is by simply asking questions: "What is it that makes you feel God is speaking?" "How might you test these thoughts and feelings?" "Is what you've heard consistent with what has been revealed in Scripture?" Such questions could be followed by briefly studying together some of the pertinent passages above.

The Spirit of God

Objectives

By the power of the Holy Spirit working through God's Word, participants will (1) identify biblical evidence regarding the Trinity, (2) recognize the Spirit's divine personhood, and (3) appreciate how Father, Son, and Holy Spirit work together for our salvation.

Opening Worship

Sing "We All Believe in One True God" (*LW* 212).

Focus

12. Read, or ask a participant to read aloud, the opening paragraph. Discuss what comes to mind upon hearing the terms *holy* and *spirit*. Such words are used frequently even by non-Christians. When combined in the Christian church, however, they take on a very specific—though perhaps not always clearly understood—meaning. Allow time for participants to relate their current understanding of the person and work of the Holy Spirit, His relation to the Father and Son, and His relationship to them personally.

A Personal Being (Inform)

13. The psalmist confesses that there is no place—on the earth, below it, or above it—in which he can escape the Spirit of God. In fact, following the format of ancient Hebrew poetry, David "parallels" God's Spirit with His presence, using these terms to describe each other. Where God is—everywhere!—there also is the Spirit.

Not only is the Holy Spirit omnipresent, being in all places; He is also omniscient, knowing all things. St. Paul notes this in 2 Corinthians when he acknowledges that the Spirit searches "all things, even the deep things of God." Omniscience and omnipresence are attributes of God alone. To ascribe them to the Holy Spirit is to claim for Him a divine status.

14. New Age and eastern religions are not alone in speaking of a vague, impersonal spirit inhabiting the world. In contrast, the Lord's Old and New Testament people have always confessed that the Spirit of God is a person. As a person, He speaks (Acts 13:2), He makes choices (1 Corinthians 12:11), and He teaches (1 Corinthians 2:13). Also, like a person—and very much unlike an impersonal energy or "life force"—He loves (Romans 15:30) and experiences grief (Isaiah 63:10).

15. In Acts 5, Peter rebukes Ananias for having "lied to the Holy Spirit." Since one could hardly lie to an inanimate or impersonal object, Peter's words reveal the apostolic belief in the Spirit's personhood. But Peter does not stop there. His condemnation goes on to reveal the true nature of this Holy Spirit to whom Ananias has lied: "You have not lied to men but to God."

St. Paul invokes the three persons of the Trinity in the benediction given to the Christians at Corinth. Even Christ Himself, in the familiar words of the Great Commission, charges His disciples to baptize "in the name of the Father and of the Son and of the Holy Spirit." The words are familiar; what may sometimes go unnoticed, however, is Jesus' use of the singular "name." Father, Son, and Holy Spirit are three persons, yet they share one and the same name, that of the almighty God Himself.

16. With regard to the Spirit's eternal relation to the Father, Jesus describes Him in John 15 as going out, or proceeding, from the Father. The Nicene Creed, however, refers to the Spirit "who proceeds from the Father *and* the Son." A comparison of Matthew 10:20 and Galatians 4:6 helps to explain this. In these passages the Holy Spirit is referred to as both "the Spirit of Your Father" and "the Spirit of His Son." Being "of" both the Father and the Son, He also proceeds from both. Such is the confession of the Athanasian Creed: "The Holy Ghost is of the Father and of the Son: neither made, nor created, nor begotten, but proceeding."

17. In John 16, Jesus describes the work of the Holy Spirit, saying that He will reveal Christ to His people by "taking from what is Mine and making it known to you." In a comparable manner, Jesus' own work is described in John 1 as that of "making known" or revealing the Father. All the Father's work has a common goal: making His love and salvation known to us through Christ, by the power of the Holy Spirit.

18. To worship God according to His nature is to worship Him as He is. He is not only the Father or the Son or the Spirit alone, but the

triune God, Father, Son, and Holy Spirit together. Therefore the church confesses in the Nicene Creed, "I believe in the Holy Ghost . . . who with the Father and the Son together is worshiped and glorified." Likewise, the church confesses in the Athanasian Creed, "the Unity in Trinity and the Trinity in Unity is to be worshiped."

A Personal Faith (Connect)

19. The Christian church does not believe in fate. Rather, the church confesses that a holy, loving, and *personal* God oversees, guides, and even intervenes in the world, the church, and the lives of its members. When Christians pray, they pray "in the Spirit" to a God who hears and answers them. Even in those times that we forget to pray or do not know what to pray, the person of the Holy Spirit is interceding and offering petitions on our behalf (Romans 8:26–27).

20. Though many people would deny the existence of spirits, demons, and angels, Scripture clearly states that they are present and active in the world. They are constantly attempting to lead us into temptation, doubt, and despair. They not only tempt us to deny God's holiness; they may also lead us to doubt that He has in fact declared us holy and continues to make us so.

Mystery and Revelation (Vision)

21. The Holy Spirit Himself reveals and instructs in God's truth. Prayerfully request that He work in the hearts and minds of those who do not believe. Furthermore, since the Spirit has inspired Scripture and continues to speak and act through this means, encourage questioning friends to seek answers in the Bible. Many of the passages found in this study may be helpful starting points for discussing the nature and work of the Spirit.

22. Though Christians frequently begin prayer in the name of the Father and end in the name of Jesus, they often pray without specific mention of the Holy Spirit. There is certainly nothing wrong with this, as Christians always pray "in the Spirit." One simple way to specifically mention the Spirit, however, would be to close prayers to our heavenly Father with the trinitarian phrase "through Jesus Christ, who lives and reigns with You and the Holy Spirit."

Life-giving Spirit

Objectives

By the power of the Holy Spirit working through God's Word, participants will (1) describe the Spirit's work, namely, giving witness to Christ and the salvation won by Him, (2) recognize the relationship between the Spirit's work of creation and re-creation, and (3) appreciate that faith itself, by which we receive our justification, is worked by the Holy Spirit.

Opening Worship

Sing "Creator Spirit, by Whose Aid" (*LW* 167).

Focus

23. Read, or ask a participant to read aloud, the opening paragraph. Discuss situations in which participants wish they had more or fewer choices to make. Prompt them to elaborate on why choice is sometimes welcome and at other times burdensome.

Breath of God (Inform)

24. Though it is sometimes assumed that the Holy Spirit was not introduced until Pentecost, the opening verses of Scripture remind us that He was present even at the time of creation. What is more, He was *active* in creation. Though we read in Genesis 2:7 that God breathed into man "the breath of life," the translators of both the Hebrew language of the Old Testament and the Greek language of the New Testament often use "breath" and "spirit" interchangeably. Since the same word is used for both, Job is able to synonymously parallel the terms in his confident confession that the "Spirit of God has made me; the breath of the Almighty gives me life." In the same manner, when reciting the Nicene Creed, the church confidently confesses its faith in "the Holy Spirit, the Lord and giver of life."

25. Though God breathed the Spirit into man at his creation, man did not long maintain his holy and "spiritual" status. In the Garden of

Eden man fell, and all since have been born in a "natural" or "fleshly," that is, sinful, state. In contrast to the life given at creation, St. Paul described death in transgressions.

Paul was not alone in proclaiming the dire consequences of man's sinful separation from the Holy Spirit. Before Paul's conversion—during a persecution of Christians to which he gave his assent!—Stephen preached the Law. Not only is natural man not endowed with the Spirit, Stephen says, but "you always resist the Holy Spirit!"

26. In David's well-known psalm of repentance, he asks that the Lord might "create in me a pure heart." It is no coincidence that David appeals to God's creative power. Creation—that which God alone can do—is precisely what must take place. Psalm 104 notes the one through whom this creative act takes place: "When you send Your Spirit, they are created." Men who are dead in sin must be brought to life, created anew. We, however, have no power to do this ourselves.

Jesus Himself explains this to His visitor Nicodemus. Just as man cannot live without first having been born, so too must he be born again, "born of water and the Spirit," if he is to enter God's kingdom. With the psalmist and with Christ, Paul declares that this takes place "through His Spirit." Only the Holy Spirit who first gave life can bestow the new and eternal life that comes with forgiveness.

27. The Gospels makes plain that Jesus was no ordinary man. Luke's Gospel, in particular, provides the details surrounding His birth, His early life, and the beginning of His earthly ministry. As these details make clear, the Holy Spirit was, from Jesus' very conception, intimately involved with His earthly life and ministry. The Holy Spirit came upon Mary that her child might truly be called the Son of God. Together with the Father, the Spirit was present at Jesus' baptism, a sign and a testimony that Jesus' ministry was divinely ordained.

The Spirit's role as a witness to Jesus' divine nature and work is later echoed in Jesus' own words. Just before His arrest, Jesus promised His disciples the Counselor, the Spirit of truth, whose work it would be to "testify about Me." This testimony, He goes on to explain, "will bring glory to Me by taking from what is Mine and making it known to you."

28. Lest we conclude that the Spirit's work stops with bearing witness to Christ, Paul explains that the Holy Spirit makes the benefits of Christ's work our own.

29. Both Scripture and the Lutheran Confessions proclaim the doctrine of "grace alone," that our justification is a free gift of God,

given by His Spirit working through the Word. They also teach the doctrine of "faith alone," that this gift of salvation is received only by faith. Paul teaches that, like grace itself, faith is a free gift of the Spirit.

Lively Spirit (Connect)

30. The assurance that we were given life by a personal and loving God, a God who breathed His own Spirit into our first parent, offers significance and meaning beyond compare. In the same manner, the promise that His Spirit is constantly at work in our lives, comforting and counseling (as His very names declare), offers us the assurance that we are certainly not alone.

31. Many find personal evangelism a difficult and, at times, frustrating task. On those occasions when we might become hesitant, nervous, or frustrated, it is comforting to know that the conversion of unbelievers does not ultimately rest upon our own words or works. Rather, the Spirit Himself is at work. It is He who testifies to Christ through our sharing of Scripture.

Live in the Spirit (Vision)

32. We are not burdened with the misconception of worship as a good work that must be done to please God. Instead, we come to hear the reassuring promise of eternal life granted in Jesus' name. We come to *receive* life in His Word and Sacraments. And we come to offer our praise and thanksgiving for this wonderful, free, certain gift of God.

33. Just as Adam did not choose to be created and we do not cooperate in our birth, neither do we have the option of taking part in our own rebirth.

The Spirit of Holiness

Objectives

By the power of the Holy Spirit working through God's Word, participants will (1) explain Christian sanctification, (2) recognize that sanctification, too, is a work of the Holy Spirit, and (3) appreciate that sanctification is worked in and through vocations.

Opening Worship

Sing "Come Down, O Love Divine" (*LW* 162).

Focus

34. Read, or ask a participant to read aloud, the opening paragraph. Discuss the current and overwhelming attention given to self-help books, videos, and programs. Ask participants to suggest reasons for their popularity. Point out that unhappiness is an inevitable consequence of sin. We—both Christians and non-Christians—are often unhappy with who we are because we are not who we were meant to be: God's holy people, created without sin to live in communion with Him.

Self-help is rarely done alone! If we need the help of others to become sober, thin, or better able to communicate with our spouse, how much more is divine assistance needed if we are to become holy?

The Helpless Self (Inform)

35. As St. Paul writes to Timothy and to the church at Rome, Scripture has many purposes. Through it the Holy Spirit teaches, rebukes, corrects, and trains in righteousness. The Spirit does this so that the Christian might be "thoroughly equipped for every good work."

36. Sanctification is an "obligation" to "put to death the misdeeds of the body." This, however, is an obligation we remain unable to fulfill by our own power. Therefore, Paul emphasizes that this putting to death is done "by the Spirit." As the misdeeds of the body are daily

put to death, Paul also explains that we are "being transformed into His [the Lord's] likeness with ever-increasing glory." This too comes not from our own power, but it "comes from the Lord, who is the Spirit."

37. Paul declares to the Corinthians who had formerly been immoral, idolaters, thieves, and drunkards: "you were washed, you were sanctified, you were justified." Paul's use of passive vocabulary cannot be overemphasized. These things were not done by the Corinthians themselves; they were done *for* them. These themes are repeated in the closing of Paul's first letter to the Thessalonian church. He prays, "May God Himself, the God of peace, sanctify you."

This reference to the One who both calls and sanctifies is reflected in the language of the Small Catechism, in which we confess that "the Holy Ghost has called me by the Gospel, enlightened me with His gifts, sanctified and kept me in the true faith."

38. In his first letter to the Corinthians, Paul explains that all who have been "baptized by one Spirit" and "given the one Spirit" are together members of this one body. In Ephesians Paul uses a different metaphor, describing the church as "God's household," a "holy temple," and a "dwelling in which God lives." Through different illustrations, Paul makes the same points. The one holy Christian church is called and gathered by the Spirit, it consists of those who have received the Holy Spirit in Baptism, and in it God continues to dwell "by His Spirit."

39. The church that has been called, gathered, enlightened, and sanctified by God Himself also desires to speak with Him who has done such great things. God, in fact, desires that we speak with Him. Therefore, His apostle exhorts Christians to pray "on all occasions," to "always keep on praying," and (in 1 Thessalonians 5:17) to "pray continually." We are told not only what to do, but also how to do it. As Paul and Jude proclaim, Christians pray "in the Holy Spirit."

This, however, is not the Spirit's only work regarding prayer. Even being strengthened by the Spirit who dwells within us, we sometimes do not know how or what to pray for. Paul's words to the Romans are infinitely encouraging. He assures his audience that "the Spirit Himself intercedes for us." Even prayer, part of the life of the sanctified Christian, is something God in His wisdom and mercy has not left to our strength alone.

40. Often when we hear the word *sanctification*, we may call to mind stereotypes of good works, such as regular church attendance or even the Boy Scout helping an elderly lady across the street. Few of us,

perhaps, immediately call to mind factory workers building tractors, technicians programming computers, or teachers at the front of a public school classroom, things not explicitly mentioned in the Law of God. Yet we read in Exodus that the gift of God's Spirit is associated with the so-called mundane tasks of masonry, carpentry, and design.

Ever-present Help (Connect)

41. Though we are assured that God, for the sake of Christ's all-sufficient death and resurrection, no longer accounts to us our sin, the Christian still daily struggles with what Scripture calls the "flesh" or the "sinful nature" that still dwells in all descendants of Adam. This daily conflict reminds us that we are not yet the entirely holy people we should be and one day will be. When this struggle becomes discouraging and disheartening—as even St. Paul recognized it to be (see Romans 7:14–24)—we can take comfort in knowing that we do not struggle alone.

42. Most Christians would agree that they ought to spend more time in prayer. Many of us fall into the trap of only remembering to whisper a hasty prayer before meals or before drifting off to sleep. Even when special effort is made to spend time with God in prayer, we sometimes simply can't find the words to pray as we would like. Because we recognize our own weakness, Paul's words in Romans 8:26–27 are a comforting reminder that our prayers are not the only ones being heard by God. The Holy Spirit Himself intercedes for us.

43. Works done in and for the congregation are not the sole means by which we live the sanctified Christian life. Being a faithful and loving spouse is a good work. Being an honest and able employee pleases God. Being an obedient child fulfills God's Law. Even in the most common acts of daily life, Christians can be confident that the Holy Spirit is at work in them and sanctifying them.

Beyond Self-Help (Vision)

44. Clarifying and explaining the Holy Spirit's necessary role in sanctification might begin most profitably with those passages that explicitly mention God as the subject of our sanctification (e.g., John 17:17; 1 Corinthians 6:11). Also, Paul's words in Romans 7:14–24 illustrate how powerless even the great apostle was to work out his own sanctification.

45. Luther's Small Catechism compiles many of the biblical passages that illustrate or explain how God's will is done through the Christian's various vocations and callings.

Baptized with the Spirit

Objectives

By the power of the Holy Spirit working through God's Word, participants will (1) identify that all baptized Christians have been baptized "in the Spirit," (2) recognize the essential relation between Christ, His Spirit, His Word, and His Baptism, and (3) appreciate the gifts and benefits bestowed in their Baptism.

Opening Worship

Sing "Baptized into Your Name Most Holy" (*LW* 224).

Focus

46. Read, or ask a participant to read aloud, the opening paragraphs. Discuss the contrasts between emotionalism and rationalism, confidence in things felt and trust in things seen. Encourage participants to explain the circumstances under which one or the other may be most appropriate and why. If participants are willing, allow them to recall episodes in which an overreliance on internal feelings or on external evidence may have resulted in less than desirable consequences.

The Promised Spirit (Inform)

47. Though the Spirit was certainly present and at work in the era of the Old Testament, the Lord promised, "on My servants, both men and women, I will pour out My Spirit." Even centuries later, however, John informs his readers that "the Spirit had not been given, since Jesus had not yet been glorified." It was not until the days before His ascension that Jesus told His disciples that they should "wait for the gift My Father promised," that "in a few days you will be baptized with the Holy Spirit" (Acts 1:5). That this promised gift was the outpouring of the Spirit is made clear a few days later—on Pentecost. Following the Spirit's dramatic entrance, the apostle Peter refers his audience to the prophet Joel to explain the morning's events (see Acts

2:16–21). Nearing the end of his impromptu sermon, Peter again makes reference to the promise of the Holy Spirit, saying this promise is "for all whom the Lord our God will call" (2:39).

48. John the Baptist prophesied that the one whose coming he announced would baptize "with the Holy Spirit." This reference to baptism with the Holy Spirit (or *in* or *by*; the English renderings are sometimes inconsistent—each translates the Greek preposition *en*) recurs in all the Gospels, the Book of Acts, and Paul's first letter to the Corinthians. While John does not specify who will be so baptized, St. Paul announces that "we were all baptized by one Spirit."

49. Though God has promised to pour out the Spirit on all of His redeemed, He has not promised to do so without means. As Peter preached to them, the Holy Spirit was received by those in the house of Cornelius. Note what Peter was preaching when this happened: "everyone who believes in Him receives forgiveness of sins through His name." Peter proclaimed the Gospel! Through God's spoken, written, and sacramental Word of grace comes God's Spirit. He has not promised to do so otherwise.

50. Just as the Holy Spirit comes with faith, so too is He inseparable from the object of our faith: Jesus Christ. Alternating his emphasis on the second and third persons of the Trinity, Paul argues in Romans that "the Spirit of God lives in you" (v. 9), that "Christ is in you" (v. 10), and twice again that the Spirit "is living in you" and "lives in you" (v. 11). This, Paul proclaims, is true of all Christians without exception.

51. The office and work of the Holy Spirit are that of proclaiming, revealing, and making present Christ and His salvation. This He does in and through the Word; this He does also in and through His work of Baptism. St. Paul declares this to be true when he explains that, being baptized into Christ, the Christian is baptized into His saving death and resurrection. The apostle Peter states even more clearly that "baptism . . . now saves you."

52. Paul urges the Ephesians to "keep the unity of the Spirit," recognizing that there is only "one body and one Spirit," only "one Lord, one faith, one baptism." This unity becomes endangered when it is stated or implied that there may be two sorts of Christians—those who have been baptized with water and those who have received an additional and immediate "baptism with the Spirit."

Comforting Spirit (Connect)

53. The church rejoices to know that God's Word does not fail, that all His promises come true, and that in Christ we are fulfilled for our benefit and for God's own glory.

54. While Christians will want at all times to avoid ranking, measuring, or comparing holiness, it comes as a great comfort to be reassured that the Holy Spirit received in Baptism is a free gift given to all of God's redeemed people, even those in whom His presence and fruits are not always obvious. The Spirit is not dependent on our holiness, our works, or even our prayer, but is poured out with water and the Word for the sake of our Lord, Jesus Christ.

55. In the last chapter of Matthew, our Lord instituted the sacrament of Christian Baptism. We can do no better—indeed, no other!—than to receive this gift according to His mandate, His institution, and His words: "in the name of the Father and of the Son and of the Holy Spirit." Members in the one holy church receive their one Holy Baptism in the name of the God who also is one and holy. In the formula for Baptism the unity in Trinity and Trinity in unity is confessed and all of His great gifts and benefits are received.

Life in the Spirit (Vision)

56. Just confess, "Jesus is Lord," and remind them that you could not make this confession without the Holy Spirit!

57. The morning and evening prayers found in Martin Luther's Small Catechism are preceded with encouragement to "bless yourself with the holy cross and say: In the name of God the Father, Son, and Holy Ghost." This sign and these words serve as a daily reminder of the Baptism with which we were received into God's household and through which we received His promised Holy Spirit, together with all His gifts and blessings.

The Fruit and Gifts of the Spirit

Objectives

By the power of the Holy Spirit working through God's Word, participants will (1) explain the nature of the Holy Spirit's fruit and gifts, (2) recognize why the Spirit's gifts are given, and (3) appreciate that the Spirit has endowed all of God's redeemed people with gifts.

Opening Worship

Sing "We Give You But Your Own" (*LW* 405).

Focus

58. Read, or ask a participant to read aloud, the opening paragraphs. Discuss the term *gifted*. Encourage participants to consider why the term is so often used in place of *able* or *talented*. It may be worth pointing out that even in its common, secular usage, the term is passive. That is, there is an implication that things such as intellect and athleticism are received from someone else rather than developed independently.

God's Gifts (Inform)

59. In describing the sanctified life that Christians live by the Spirit, Paul describes some of the fruit produced in believers. "Against such things," he writes, "there is no law." In fact, such things, when performed by those regenerated by the Spirit, are a fulfillment of God's holy Law. The Christian, however, having been raised to new life by the Spirit, no longer lives under the Law (see Galatians 5:18).

In his letter to the Romans, Paul reminds us that our sanctification is never complete in this life. Though we exhibit in our lives the fruit of the Spirit who sanctifies us, these are only "firstfruits." Until we are finally made entirely pure and holy upon our arrival in God's heavenly presence, we continue to "groan inwardly" and "wait eagerly" for our final redemption.

60. First, as noted in Romans, Christians do not necessarily have the same gifts. They do, however, regardless of their gift or gifts, have the same Spirit (1 Corinthians 12:4).

Second, it should be noted that even while the above lists were given by the same author—and the Corinthian lists even to the same audience—Paul never enumerates precisely the same gifts. Nor does he even clarify what he means by particular gifts.

61. The gifts that come with sanctification are very different from the Gift given for our justification. Christ gave His life, as we confess in the Nicene Creed, "for us men, and for our salvation." Spiritual gifts, however, are not given for our own personal benefit, but for the good of others. Paul, who has the most to say about spiritual gifts, insists that they are to be used "for the common good" of the church. Likewise, Peter exhorts Christians to use their gifts "to serve others."

62. The Corinthian church was, when Paul wrote, a complete mess. It was divided by factions. It was tolerant of sexual immorality unheard of even among pagans. Members were suing one another, and there were disputes concerning marriage, worship, and the Lord's Supper. And yet Paul begins his first letter by claiming that the Christians at Corinth "do not lack any spiritual gift." How could he say such a thing? He could say such a thing, as he later explains by way of repetition, because the gifts of the spirit are given "to each one" in the Christian church. All those who have been baptized have received the Holy Spirit together with His gifts.

63. It may at first strike us as strange that Paul would consider the ability to teach, encourage, lead, administer, help, or serve as a "spiritual" gift. As we well know, there are many "unspiritual" people in the world who are quite competent teachers and administrators. There are plenty of non-Christians who still go out of their way to encourage, help, and serve others. These do not seem to be in any way supernatural gifts; they seem to be talents exercised even by some who have not received the Holy Spirit.

Remember that all we have—our goods, our health, our talents and abilities—we have as a gift from God. Rather than assuming that the adjective *spiritual* refers to the nature of the gifts that Paul describes, we might more readily conclude that it refers to the source of these gifts, that is, the God who "is spirit" (John 4:24).

64. Just as "the wind blows wherever it pleases," Jesus explains that the activity of the Holy Spirit is in some ways incomprehensible. Paul reiterates Jesus' thought when he declares that the Spirit gives His

gifts "just as He determines." Recognizing this, the church is also reminded that the gifts of the Spirit are precisely that: gifts. We can only receive them as they are given. We dare not demand that God give, or even assume that He gives, Christians today all of the gifts that He once gave to the apostolic church.

Gifts of Service (Connect)

65. Many of us may fall into that category of people who were not considered "gifted" children. We were not born with certain outstanding abilities that the world admires. But we have been born anew, we have been made God's children, and He certainly considers us gifted. There is great comfort in knowing that our heavenly Father knows our true worth and that He makes use of our gifts for His own glory.

66. When we are at times tempted to envy the gifts of others, Paul's words in 1 Corinthians 12 are a great encouragement. He reminds us that "the body is not made up of one part, but of many" (v. 14) and that "God has arranged the parts in the body, every one of them, just as He wanted them to be" (v. 18). No matter what our gifts or how seemingly unspectacular, we can be assured that they are precisely those that God meant us to have.

Gifted Children (Vision)

67. The Spirit gives His good gifts, as St. Paul declares, "just as He determines" (1 Corinthians 12:11). We are not at leisure to dictate what gifts are given, when, and to whom. Instead, we can only rejoice to be assured that God's wisdom is greater than our own, that He distributes His gifts for His glory and for the benefit of the church.

Also remember that, being gifts, these are given freely and with no merit on our part. That is, they are not rewards. Nor are they a means by which to determine if some are "more holy" than others. In Baptism, all Christians receive the Holy Spirit together with the full and sufficient forgiveness of sins. On this basis alone—not on account of any other gifts, talents, or abilities—we are reckoned holy.

Appendix of Lutheran Teaching

Apology of the Augsburg Confession

Philip Melanchthon, a lay associate of Dr. Martin Luther, wrote the apology to clarify for Emperor Charles V just what Lutherans believed. Melanchthon summarized Lutheran teaching from the Bible and addressed the controversies of his day. This apology remains a standard of Lutheran teaching.

VII & VIII. 13–16, 22: Of the Church

For it is necessary to understand what it is that principally makes us members, and that, living members, of the Church. If we will define the Church only as an outward polity of the good and wicked, men will not understand that the kingdom of Christ is righteousness of heart and the gift of the Holy Ghost [that the kingdom of Christ is spiritual, as nevertheless it is; that therein Christ inwardly rules, strengthens, and comforts heart, and imparts the Holy Ghost and various spiritual gifts], but they will judge that it is only the outward observance of certain forms of worship and rites. Likewise, what difference will there be between the people of the Law and the Church if the Church is an outward polity? But Paul distinguishes the Church from the people of the Law thus, that the Church is a spiritual people, *i.e.,* that it has been distinguished from the heathen not by civil rites [not in the polity and civil affairs], but that it is the true people of God, regenerated by the Holy Ghost. Among the people of the Law, apart from the promise of Christ, also the carnal seed [all those who by nature were born Jews and Abraham's seed] had promises concerning corporeal things, of government, etc. And because of these even the wicked among them were called the people of God, because God had separated this carnal seed from other nations by certain outward ordinances and promises; and yet, these wicked persons did not please God. But the Gospel [which is preached in the Church] brings not merely the shadow of eternal things, but the eternal things themselves, the Holy Ghost and righteousness, by which we are righteous before God. [But every true

Christian is even here upon earth partaker of eternal blessings, even of eternal comfort, of eternal life, and of the Holy Ghost, and of righteousness which is from God, until he will be completely saved in the world to come.]

Therefore, only those are the people, according to the Gospel, who receive this promise of the Spirit. Besides, the Church is the kingdom of Christ, distinguished from the kingdom of the devil. It is certain, however, that the wicked are in the power of the devil, and members of the kingdom of the devil, as Paul teaches, Eph. 2, 2, when he says that the devil *now worketh in the children of disobedience.* And Christ says to the Pharisees, who certainly had outward fellowship with the Church, *i.e.,* with the saints among the people of the Law (for they held office, sacrificed, and taught): *Ye are of your father, the devil,* John 8, 44. Therefore, the Church, which is truly the kingdom of Christ, is properly the congregation of saints. For the wicked are ruled by the devil, and are captives of the devil; they are not ruled by the Spirit of Christ. (*Triglotta,* p. 231)

The Smalcald Articles of 1537

To prepare for a general church council, some German princes asked Dr. Martin Luther to draw up a statement of faith. These articles, which dealt with Christian teaching and specific controversies, gained popularity and became a standard of Lutheran teaching.

Part III, art. III.1–8, 40: Of Repentance

This office [of the Law] the New Testament retains and urges, as St. Paul, Rom. 1, 18, does, saying: *The wrath of God is revealed from heaven against all ungodliness and unrighteousness of men.* Again, 3, 19: *All the world is guilty before God. No man is righteous before Him.* And Christ says, John 16, 8: *The Holy Ghost will reprove the world of sin.*

This, then, is the thunderbolt of God by which He strikes in a heap [hurls to the ground] both manifest sinners and false saints [hypocrites], and suffers no one to be in the right [declares no one righteous], but drives them all together to terror and despair. This is the hammer, as Jeremiah says, 23, 29: *Is not My Word like a hammer that breaketh the rock in pieces?* This is not *activa contritio* or manufactured repentance, but *passiva contritio* [torture of conscience], true sorrow of heart, suffering and sensation of death.

This, then, is what it means to begin true repentance; and here man must hear such a sentence as this: Your are all of no account, whether you be manifest sinners or saints [in your own opinion]; you all must become different and do otherwise than you now are and are doing [no matter what sort of people you are], whether you are as great, wise, powerful, and holy as you may. Here no one is [righteous, holy], godly, etc.

But to this office the New Testament immediately adds the consolatory promise of grace through the Gospel, which must be believed, as Christ declares, Mark 1, 15: *Repent and believe the Gospel, i.e.,* become different and do otherwise, and believe My promise. And John, preceding Him, is called a preacher of repentance, however, for the remission of sins, *i.e.,* John was to accuse all, and convict them of being sinners, that they might know what they were before God, and might acknowledge that they were lost men, and might thus be prepared for the Lord, to receive grace, and to expect and accept from Him the remission of sins. Thus also Christ Himself says, Luke 24, 47: *Repentance and remission of sins must be preached in My name among all nations.*

But whenever the Law alone, without the Gospel being added, exercises this its office, there is [nothing else than] death and hell, and man must despair, like Saul and Judas; *Through sin the Law killeth.* On the other hand, the Gospel brings consolation and remission, not only in one way, but through the Word and Sacraments, and the like, as we shall hear afterward in order that [thus] there is *with the Lord plenteous redemption,* as Ps. 130, 7 says, against the dreadful captivity of sin.

. . . [But] in Christians [genuine] repentance continues until death, because, through the entire life it contends with sin remaining in the flesh, as Paul, Rom. 7,14–25, [shows] testifies that he *wars with the law in his members,* etc.; and that, not by his own powers, but by the gift of the Holy Ghost that follows the remission of sins. This gift daily cleanses and sweeps out the remaining sins, and works so as to render man truly pure and holy. (*Triglotta,* pp. 479, 481, 489)

Formula of Concord

Following Luther's death in 1546, confusion disrupted the Lutheran churches. Some wished to compromise on matters of doctrine in order to attain greater peace and unity with Calvinists and Roman Catholics. Others claimed to be true Lutherans but strayed from

Luther's teaching. In 1576 Elector August of Saxony called a conference to clarify the issues. The result was the Formula of Concord (*concord* means "unity"), published in 1580.

Epitome II.2–6: Of Free Will

1. Concerning this subject, our doctrine, faith, and confession is, that in spiritual things the understanding and reason of man are [altogether] blind, and by their own powers understand nothing, as it is written 1 Cor. 2, 14: *The natural man receiveth not the things of the Spirit of God, for they are foolishness to him; neither can he know them when he is examined concerning spiritual things.*

2. Likewise we believe, teach, and confess that the unregenerate will of man is not only turned away from God, but also has become an enemy of God, so that it only has an inclination and desire for that which is evil and contrary to God, as it is written Gen. 8, 21: *The imagination of man's heart is evil from his youth.* Also Rom. 8, 7: *The carnal mind is enmity against God; for it is not subject to the Law of God, neither, indeed, can be.* Yea, as little as a dead body can quicken itself to bodily, earthly life, so little can man, who by sin is spiritually dead, raise himself to spiritual life, as it is written Eph. 2, 5: *Even when we were dead in sins, He hath quickened us together with Christ;* 2 Cor. 3, 5: *Not that we are sufficient of ourselves to think anything good as of ourselves, but that we are sufficient is of God.*

3. God the Holy Ghost, however, does not effect conversion without means, but uses for this purpose the preaching and hearing of God's Word, as it is written Rom. 1, 16: *The Gospel is the power of God unto salvation to every one that believeth.* Also Rom. 10, 17: *Faith cometh by hearing of the Word of God.* And it is God's will that His Word should be heard, and that man's ears should not be closed. Ps. 95, 8. With this Word the Holy Ghost is present, and opens hearts, so that they, as Lydia in Acts 16, 14, are attentive to it, and are thus converted alone through the grace and power of the Holy Ghost, whose work alone the conversion of man is. For without His grace, and if He do not grant the increase, our willing and running, our planting, sowing, and watering, all are nothing, as Christ says John 15, 5: *Without Me ye can do nothing.* With these brief words He denies to the free will its powers, and ascribes everything to God's grace, in order that no one may boast before God. 1 Cor. 1, 29; 2 Cor. 12, 5; 2 Cor. 12, 5; Jer. 9, 23. (*Triglotta,* p. 787).

Thorough Declaration II.56, 58–60: Of Free Will

For concerning the presence, operation, and gifts of the Holy Ghost we should not and cannot always judge *ex sensu* [from feeling], as to how and when they are experienced in the heart; but because they are often covered and occur in great weakness, we should be certain from, and according to, the promise, that the Word of God preached and heard is [truly] an office and work of the Holy Ghost, by which He is certainly efficacious and works in our hearts, 2 Cor. 2, 14ff.; 3, 5 ff.

. . . But when such a person despises the instrument of the Holy Ghost, and will not hear, no injustice is done to him if the Holy Ghost does not enlighten him, but allows him to remain in the darkness of his unbelief and to perish; for regarding this matter it is written: *How often would I have gathered thy children together, even as a hen gathereth her chickens under her wings; and ye would not!* Matt. 23, 37.

And in this respect it may well be said that man is not a stone or block. For a stone or block does not resist the person who moves it, nor does it understand and is sensible of what is being done with it, as man with his will so long resists God the Lord until he is [has been] converted. And it is nevertheless true that man before his conversion is still a rational creature, having an understanding and will, however, not an understanding with respect to divine things, or a will to will something good and salutary. Yet he can do nothing whatever towards his conversion (as has also been said [frequently] above), and is in this respect much worse than a stone and block; for he resists the Word and will of God, until God awakens him from the death of sin, enlightens and renews him.

And although God does not force man to become godly (for those who always resist the Holy Ghost and persistently oppose the known truth, as Stephen says of the hardened Jews, Acts 7, 51, are not converted), yet God the Lord draws the man whom He wishes [decreed] to convert, and draws him in such a way that his darkened understanding is turned into an enlightened one and his perverse will into an obedient one. And this [just this] is what the Scriptures call *creating a new heart,* Ps. 51, 10. (*Triglotta,* pp. 903, 905)

Glossary

calling. See **vocation**.

charismatics. From the Greek word *charismata*, meaning "gift." Charismatics share the belief of Pentecostals that God "baptizes" people with the Holy Spirit today by bestowing miraculous gifts/abilities, such as speaking in tongues, prophesying, and healing.

external Word. An expression used by Luther to describe the Bible and biblical teaching. Luther contrasted the external Word with the internal word or feelings sought by people who believed that the Spirit guided them directly, apart from the Bible.

filioque. Literally, "and the Son." This phrase was added to the Nicene Creed in the West to emphasize that the Holy Spirit proceeds from the Father *and the Son*. See page 18.

holy. Set apart for a divine purpose (e.g., Holy Scripture is set apart from all other types of writing). The Holy Spirit makes Christians holy (see **sanctification**).

inerrancy. The teaching that the Bible, as originally inspired by the Holy Spirit and recorded by the prophets, apostles, and evangelists, did not contain errors. Churches that teach inerrancy recognize that scribes and translators have erred in copying the Bible over the centuries.

inspiration. Guidance by a spirit. In many religions the term describes a trancelike state of spirit possession. In Christianity the term usually describes the guidance of God's Holy Spirit provided to the prophets and the writers of the Bible.

justification. God declares sinners to be just or righteous for Christ's sake; that is, God has imputed or charged our sins to Christ, and He imputes or credits Christ's righteousness to us.

means of grace. The means by which God gives us the forgiveness, life, and salvation won by the death and resurrection of Christ: the Gospel, Baptism, and the Lord's Supper.

original sin. The corruption and guilt all people have inherited from Adam and Eve. Original sin causes a person to commit "actual" sins.

perfectionism. The belief that Christians can attain perfect sinlessness in this life. The teaching is popular in the Wesleyan and Anabaptist traditions. Roman Catholics have taught a form of perfectionism to describe the holiness of the saints.

polemical. From the Greek word for "battle." The term describes conversation or writing that attacks and refutes.

regeneration. From a Latin word meaning "rebirth." The Holy Spirit gives new life through Baptism and God's Word.

sacrament. Literally, "something sacred." In the Lutheran church a sacrament is a sacred act that (1) was instituted by God, (2) has a visible element, and (3) offers the forgiveness of sins earned by Christ. The sacraments include Baptism, the Lord's Supper, and Absolution (if one counts the person speaking absolution as the visible element; Large Catechism IV.74; Apology XIII. 4–5).

sanctification. The spiritual growth that follows justification by grace through faith in Christ.

speaking in tongues. A Semitic expression used in the Bible to mean "speaking in foreign languages." See Nehemiah 13:24; Isaiah 28:11; and Acts 2:4.

vocation. From the Latin word for "calling." A person's occupation or duties before God. For example, a person may serve as a father, a husband, and an engineer. Each "calling" comes with different responsibilities.